For Chocolate Lovers

FROM TRUFFLES TO TIRAMISU

THE TANNER BROTHERS

with photography by Peter Cassidy

CASTLE BOOKS

This edition published in 2011 by
CASTLE BOOKS (R)
a division of BOOK SALES, INC.
276 Fifth Avenue Suite 206
New York, New York 10001
USA

This edition published by arrangement with Jacqui Small, an imprint of Aurum
Press Limited, 7 Greenland St, London, NW1 0ND

First published in 2006 by Jacqui Small

Publisher Jacqui Small
Managing Editor Nicola Graimes
Art Director Ashley Western
Stylist Roisin Nield
Production Peter Colley

ISBN-13: 978-0-7858-2764-1

10 9 8 7 6 5 4 3 2 1

Printed and bound in China

Page 1: *Chocolate tiramisu*
Page 2: Chocolate brownies

Contents

Chocolate is pure comfort food to us. From our first mouthful as children – we were always first in the line to lick the spoon – to making decadent desserts in our restaurant and brasserie, chocolate is something we have always loved and enjoyed.

Dark, milk, or white chocolate can be made into wonderful sweet or savory dishes. The great taste of chocolate is due to its cocoa content, the higher the percentage of cocoa the richer, stronger, and more bitter the flavor. Using good quality chocolate you can create a fantastic range of flavors: tarts that melt in the mouth; chocolate truffles that are silky and smooth; intensely rich and decadent sauces; or delicate and light mousses.

This wonderful ancient ingredient can be paired with fruits, nuts, meats, and cheese, so we have put together some of our favorite recipes to show you how versatile chocolate is and how to create fantastic results in your own kitchen. We hope our recipes bring you the pleasure they have to us.

Types of chocolate

When choosing chocolate to cook with, opt for one with a high percentage of cocoa solids and no more than 31 percent cocoa butter. Bear in mind that over 75 percent cocoa solids gives an extra bitter, very dark chocolate that some people find unpalatable.

Bittersweet and semisweet chocolate, with a cocoa solids content of between 55 and 75 percent, has a rich, full taste, and the majority of the recipes in this book use a chocolate that falls within this range. It is advisable to always buy the best quality you can find, and generally the higher the cocoa content the more expensive the chocolate will be. Semisweet chocolate contains more sugar than bittersweet.

Couverture chocolate is a professional quality coating chocolate containing a proportion of cocoa butter (about 32 percent), which makes it extremely glossy and easy to work with. It is available from specialty candy-making shops and is used for confectionery and decorations.

Milk chocolate has added milk solids or cream and sugar. Quality varies, so again it is best to buy a more expensive brand and avoid those with added vegetable fat.

White chocolate is not technically chocolate at all but a combination of cocoa butter, milk solids, and sugar.

Melting Chocolate

Chocolate should be melted carefully and gently. If overheated it can scorch or, if it comes into contact with water or steam, can "seize" when it hardens into a lump making it unworkable.

First, break the chocolate into small, even-sized pieces and place in a heatproof bowl that is clean and dry. Place the bowl over a saucepan half-filled with gently simmering water. (The bowl should not touch the water.) The heat should be at its lowest setting or turned off. Stir frequently to keep the temperature steady until the chocolate is melted.

Tempering

Tempering is a method of melting and cooling chocolate to a certain temperature so that when it cools it has a glossy luster and a great "snap" when broken. Tempering is necessary when making filled chocolates, chocolate decorations, or coating, but make sure you use good quality chocolate. It is best to work in a cool, dry environment.

A simple way to temper chocolate is to melt the chocolate following the method on page 7 until it reaches a temperature of 115°F. Remove the bowl from the heat then pour two-thirds on to a dry marble slab or work surface. Using a spatula, spread the chocolate back and fourth until it thickens and is on the point of setting. Transfer the chocolate from the marble to the reserved melted chocolate, and stir until combined.

Chocolate decorations

Bubble wrap chocolate

This is a simple yet stunning way to decorate desserts and cakes.

$3^{1}/_{2}$oz bittersweet or semisweet chocolate, broken into pieces

1 Melt the chocolate in a heatproof bowl placed over a saucepan of gently simmering water.

2 Place a 6-inch square sheet of plastic bubble wrap (bubble-side up) on a baking sheet. Pour the melted chocolate over the sheet and spread out using a spatula. Chill until set. Carefully remove the plastic from the chocolate then break into pieces the desired size.

Making chocolate curls and shavings

Decorative curls can be made from chocolate that is at room temperature. Use a vegetable peeler to shave the sides of a block or bar of white, milk, or bittersweet or semisweet chocolate. For shavings, use chilled chocolate and follow the method above.

White and milk chocolate garnish

Swirls of melted white chocolate over milk chocolate (or you could use bittersweet or semisweet) give a highly decorative effect. Leave to set in sheets then break into pieces the desired size.

9oz milk or bittersweet chocolate, broken into pieces

$1^3/_4$oz white chocolate, broken into pieces

1 Melt the milk chocolate in a heatproof bowl placed over a saucepan of gently simmering water. Repeat this method with the white chocolate.

2 Line a baking sheet with baking parchment. Pour the milk chocolate over the sheet and spread out evenly using a spatula.

3 Using a spoon, drizzle the white chocolate over the dark chocolate in a liberal pattern. Chill until set then break into pieces. Chill until ready to use.

Chocolate filigree

Ornamental shapes and decorations add the finishing touch to desserts and cakes.

5 tbsp all-purpose flour
$1/_2$ cup confectioners' sugar
scant $1/_2$ cup cocoa powder
scant $1/_4$ cup egg whites

1 Preheat the oven to 375°F. Line a large baking sheet with baking parchment. Sift the flour, confectioners' sugar, and cocoa powder together into a mixing bowl then beat in the egg whites.

2 Spoon the chocolate mixture into a pastry bag then cut a small hole at the end. Pipe the mixture into your desired design on to the baking parchment.

3 Bake for 3–4 minutes until set. Remove from the oven and leave the decorations to cool slightly then carefully transfer to a wire rack to cool.

Piped chocolate decorations

Melted chocolate can be piped into decorative patterns to enhance desserts and special occasion cakes.

For this, gently pour cooled melted or tempered chocolate into a baking parchment pastry bag or small plastic pastry bag and cut a very small piece off the end.

Use as desired, or if it is your first attempt it is advisable to draw a pattern on to a sheet of baking parchment then trace over the top with the piped chocolate. Leave to set, either at room temperature or chill. Carefully remove from the paper using a spatula.

Hot desserts

Banana and chocolate soufflé pancakes

THESE IRRESISTIBLE PANCAKES ARE VERY STRAIGHTFORWARD TO MAKE. THE FILLING IS EXTREMELY LIGHT AND AIRY WITH THE ADDED BONUS OF MELTED CHOCOLATE.

Ingredients
1 generous cup all-purpose flour
a pinch of salt
1 standard egg, lightly beaten
1 tbsp unsalted butter, melted
1¼ cups milk
light olive oil or sunflower oil, for frying
confectioners' sugar, for dusting

For the filling:
8 standard egg whites
¼ cup superfine sugar
1 quantity crème pâtissière (see page 18)
7oz bittersweet or semisweet chocolate, broken
  into pieces
4 bananas, sliced

Serves 6

1 To make the pancakes, sift the flour and salt into a mixing bowl. Make a well in the center and whisk in the whole eggs, butter, and half the milk. Whisk to make a smooth batter, then mix in the remaining milk. Leave the batter to rest for 20 minutes.

2 Preheat the oven to 427°F. Heat a 7-inch non-stick skillet to a high temperature – you should feel the heat rising. Pour in 1 teaspoon of oil and swirl it around the pan. Ladle 2–3 tablespoons of batter into the skillet and swirl it around until it coats the base of the pan. Cook until light golden, about 1½ minutes, then flip it over and cook for a further 45 seconds. Transfer to a plate. Repeat this process to make 12 pancakes in total.

3 To make the soufflé, whisk the egg whites until they form soft peaks. Add the superfine sugar, a little at a time, and whisk until the mixture forms stiff peaks. Whisk half the egg white mixture into the crème pâtissière then fold in the remaining mixture using a metal spoon.

4 Place a pancake on a baking sheet and top one half with a good spoonful of the soufflé mixture, leaving a gap around the edge, then place a few slices of banana and some chocolate pieces on top. Fold the other half of the pancake over and repeat with the remaining pancakes. Bake for 8–10 minutes. Serve 2 pancakes per person, dusting the tops with confectioners' sugar.

Warm chocolate cake

TAKE CARE NOT TO OVERCOOK THESE LIGHT CHOCOLATE CAKES – THE CENTERS SHOULD OOZE WHEN CUT INTO.

Ingredients
4½oz bittersweet or semisweet chocolate, broken into pieces
9 tbsp unsalted butter, plus extra for greasing
4 standard eggs
6 tbsp superfine sugar
½ cup self-rising flour, plus extra for dusting
1 tbsp cocoa powder, plus extra for dusting
whipped cream, to serve (optional)

Serves 6

1 Melt the chocolate and butter together in a heatproof bowl placed over a saucepan of gently simmering water. Stir until combined then leave to cool.

2 Preheat the oven to 350°F and lightly butter and flour six scant 1-cup ramekins. Whisk the eggs and sugar together until light and pale and doubled in volume.

3 Fold the egg mixture into the cooled chocolate. Sift in the flour and cocoa then fold until combined.

4 Spoon the chocolate mixture into the prepared ramekins and bake for 6–7 minutes until risen. Loosen the puddings with a knife and carefully turn out. Dust with cocoa powder and serve with whipped cream, if using.

Previous page: Banana and chocolate soufflé pancakes
Opposite: Warm chocolate cake

Ingredients

2 tbsp superfine sugar
$\frac{1}{4}$ cup water
9oz white chocolate, broken into pieces
2 tbsp almond liqueur
4 standard egg yolks
juice and zest of 2 mandarins
2 tbsp orange liqueur
$\frac{2}{3}$ cup heavy cream
$\frac{1}{4}$ cup confectioners' sugar
1 vanilla bean, split and seeds scraped out
4 pieces of bittersweet chocolate garnish (see page 9)
Devonshire cream, to serve

For the spiced bread:
1 standard egg, lightly beaten
$\frac{2}{3}$ cup milk
2 tbsp light cream
scant $\frac{1}{2}$ cup confectioners' sugar
2 tbsp butter
pain d'épice or brioche, cut into six $2\frac{1}{2}$- x 2-inch
   thick slices

Serves 6

1 Heat the sugar and water in a small saucepan, stirring, until the sugar dissolves. Bring the mixture to a boil and cook until it becomes syrupy. Set aside to cool.

2 Melt the chocolate in a heatproof bowl placed over a saucepan of gently simmering water – take care not to overheat the chocolate as it can separate. Leave to cool.

3 Put the sugar syrup, almond liqueur, and egg yolks in a bowl placed over a saucepan of gently simmering water and whisk until light and fluffy. Remove from the heat and leave to cool. Fold the mixture into the melted chocolate. Add the mandarin juice and zest, and stir in the orange liqueur.

4 Lightly whip the cream with the confectioners' sugar and vanilla seeds then fold into the chocolate mixture.

5 To make the spiced bread, mix the egg with the milk, cream, and confectioners' sugar. Melt the butter in a skillet. Dip each piece of bread into the cream mixture then fry until golden brown.

6 To serve, place a round of bread in the bottom of a shallow bowl, pour the chocolate soup over the top and brown under the broiler (or use a blowtorch) for a few seconds. Top the bread with a piece of chocolate and serve with a scoop of Devonshire cream.

Warm spice bread with white chocolate-mandarin sauce

WE WERE GIVEN THIS RECIPE BY OUR GOOD FRIEND ADAM NEWELL, WHO IS CHEF/PATRON AT "ZIBIBBO" IN WELLINGTON, NEW ZEALAND. THE "SOUP" IS LIGHT, FLUFFY AND VERY RICH AND GOES REALLY WELL WITH THE SPICED BREAD. TOP WITH DEVONSHIRE CREAM.

1 Preheat the oven to 350°F. Lightly butter 4 large ramekins or ovenproof mugs and set aside.

2 Break the brioche into small pieces and divide between the ramekins or mugs.

3 Gently heat the milk with the vanilla bean and seeds, add 5½oz of the chocolate and stir until it melts.

4 Whisk together the eggs and sugar then add the chocolate milk, stirring well.

5 Divide the remaining chocolate between the ramekins or mugs, pour over the hot chocolate milk, and press the brioche down so that it absorbs the liquid. Leave to stand for 2 minutes.

6 Put the ramekins or mugs in a roasting pan. Pour in enough hot water to come two-thirds of the way up the sides of the ramekins or mugs. Bake for 30–40 minutes then leave to rest for 10 minutes. Serve with a good spoonful of Devonshire or whipped cream, if using. (You can also turn the puddings out of the ramekins or mugs.)

Chocolate brioche butter pudding

THIS TAKE ON THE CLASSIC BREAD AND BUTTER PUDDING USES BRIOCHE AND CHOCOLATE, WHICH GIVES IT REAL GUTS. A DOLLOP OF DEVONSHIRE CREAM FINISHES IT OFF TO PERFECTION!

Ingredients
butter, for greasing
7oz brioche, about 6 slices
2½ cups milk
1 vanilla bean, split and seeds scraped out
7oz bittersweet or semisweet chocolate, broken into pieces
4 free-range eggs
2 tbsp superfine sugar
Devonshire or whipped cream, to serve (optional)

Serves 4

1 Preheat the oven to 350°F. Line a 12in square x 2in deep baking pan with baking parchment.

2 Melt the chocolate and butter together in a heatproof bowl placed over a saucepan of gently simmering water. Stir well until the chocolate and butter are mixed together. Dissolve the coffee in 1 tablespoon water then stir into the chocolate mixture.

3 Using an electric hand whisk, whisk the eggs and sugar together in a heatproof bowl placed over a pan of gently simmering water until doubled in volume. (This is called a sabayon and it is ready when light and pale and the mixture holds a ribbon trail for 4 seconds when the whisk is lifted.)

4 Remove from the heat and gently fold in the chocolate mixture. Sift in the flour a little at a time, folding it in as you go. Finally, fold in the nuts.

5 Spoon the chocolate mixture into the prepared baking pan, level the top and bake for 25–30 minutes until risen. Leave to cool slightly then cut into squares. Serve warm with cream or ice cream, if liked.

Chocolate brownies

THIS CLASSIC CHOCOLATE BROWNIE RECIPE COMES FROM OUR TIME IN NEW YORK – EVERY BITE BRINGS BACK HAPPY MEMORIES.

Ingredients
1lb 3oz bittersweet or semisweet chocolate, broken into pieces
11½oz unsalted butter, cut into pieces
1 tbsp instant coffee granules
5 large free-range eggs
1⅔ cups superfine sugar
1½ cups all-purpose flour
scant 1 cup walnuts, chopped
scant 1 cup macadamia nuts, chopped
cream or vanilla ice cream, to serve (optional)

Makes about 16

Pictured on page 2

1 Put the milk, half of the sugar, and vanilla bean and seeds in a saucepan, and gently warm. Remove from the heat and leave to infuse for 15 minutes.

2 In a mixing bowl, whisk together the egg yolks, the flour, and the remaining sugar until it forms a smooth paste.

3 Pour the milk over and mix well. Transfer to a clean pan and heat gently for 10–15 minutes, stirring continuously, until the mixture begins to thicken. Transfer to a clean bowl, cover with plastic wrap and leave to cool.

4 Preheat the oven to 400°F. Brush the insides of 6 large ramekin dishes with soft butter – always brush up the sides. Add a tablespoon of sugar to each ramekin and tilt and rotate until the inside is coated in the sugar. Pour out any excess sugar then chill.

5 Whisk the egg whites until they form stiff peaks. Put the crème pâtissière into a large bowl and whisk well. Add half the egg whites and whisk well until the mixture forms a smooth paste. Add the remaining egg whites and fold in with a large metal spoon.

6 Spoon the soufflé mixture into the prepared ramekins, filling them up to the top. Carefully tap down the dishes (this releases any trapped air). Place on a baking sheet and bake for 10–15 minutes – do not open the oven door during cooking since this allows the hot air to escape.

7 Meanwhile, make the chocolate sauce. Gently bring the cream up to a boil. Add the chocolate and stir until melted. Set aside.

8 When the soufflés are ready, carefully but quickly remove from the oven. Dust with cocoa powder and serve immediately with the chocolate sauce.

Ingredients

For the crème pâtissière:
2 cups milk
generous $1/2$ cup superfine sugar, plus extra for dusting
1 vanilla bean, split and seeds scraped out
6 standard eggs, separated
$1/2$ cup all-purpose flour
softened butter, for greasing

For the chocolate sauce:
$1^1/2$ cups heavy cream
$5^1/2$oz bittersweet or semisweet chocolate
cocoa powder, for dusting

Serves 6

Vanilla soufflé with chocolate sauce

A SUPERB, BREATH-TAKING DESSERT WITH A GUARANTEED "WOW" FACTOR. THE SECRETS TO A GOOD SOUFFLÉ ARE A WELL-BUTTERED AND -SUGARED DISH, THE CRÈME PÂTISSIÈRE SHOULD ALWAYS BE AT ROOM TEMPERATURE, AND THE MIXING BOWL METICULOUSLY CLEAN AND, MOST IMPORTANTLY, GOOD COMPANY TO SHARE IT WITH.

Ice creams and chilled sweets

Dark chocolate ice cream

THERE IS NOTHING BETTER THAN THE TASTE OF HOMEMADE ICE CREAM, AND THIS RECIPE IS BOTH RICH AND ABSOLUTELY DELICIOUS.

Ingredients

2 standard eggs, plus 2 additional yolks
generous 1/2 cup superfine sugar
2 1/2 cups heavy cream
7oz bittersweet or semisweet chocolate, broken
  into pieces

Makes about 3 cups

1 Whisk the eggs, additional yolks, and sugar together until light and pale.

2 Put half the heavy cream into a saucepan and bring up to a boil. Pour the cream over the chocolate and stir until it is melted. Leave to cool.

3 When cool, pour the chocolate and cream mixture into the egg mixture. Pour into a clean saucepan and heat gently, stirring constantly, until the mixture is thick enough to coat the back of a wooden spoon; do not allow it to boil or the mixture will curdle. Pass through a fine sieve into a bowl and leave to cool.

4 Fold the chocolate mixture into the remaining heavy cream. Pour the mixture into an ice cream maker and churn then freeze. If making by hand, pour the mixture into a freezer-proof container then freeze for 40 minutes. Remove from the freezer, whisk to break up any ice crystals then refreeze. Repeat this process for the next 2 1/2 hours then freeze until firm.

5 Leave the ice cream to soften for 5–10 minutes then serve in scoops.

Chocolate mousse

WE HAVE EXPERIMENTED WITH MANY MOUSSE RECIPES AND AGREE THAT THIS IS ONE OF THE MOST DELICIOUS AND SIMPLE TO MAKE.

Ingredients

5 1/2oz bittersweet or semisweet chocolate, broken
  into pieces
5 standard egg whites
3/4 cup heavy cream, whipped
cocoa powder and confectioners' sugar, for dusting

Serves 4

1 Melt the chocolate in a heatproof bowl placed over a saucepan of gently simmering water. Leave to cool slightly.

2 Whisk the egg whites until they form soft peaks then fold into the chocolate. Fold the whipped cream into the chocolate mixture. Chill until set.

3 To serve, dust each serving plate with cocoa powder and confectioners' sugar then shape the mousse between 2 warm dessertspoons into a quenelle or egg-shaped portion. Place 3 quenelles on each plate and serve. Alternatively, spoon the mousse into tall glasses and chill until set.

Previous page: Dark chocolate ice cream
Opposite: Chocolate mousse

White chocolate and chili ice cream

THE MOUTH-TINGLING, CLEAN FLAVOR OF THE RED JALAPEÑO CHILI WORKS WELL WITH THE WHITE CHOCOLATE IN THIS BRILLIANT AND UNUSUAL ICE CREAM THAT HAS BECOME A BIG FAVORITE AT OUR RESTAURANT.

1 Bring the water to a boil in a saucepan. Add 1 tablespoon of the superfine sugar and the chili then reduce the heat and simmer for 5 minutes until it becomes a light syrup. Remove from the heat and allow to cool.

2 Put the cream, milk, and vanilla bean in a saucepan and bring up to a boil. Remove from the heat and allow to infuse and cool.

3 Melt the chocolate in a heatproof bowl placed over a saucepan of gently simmering water. Leave to cool.

4 Whisk the egg yolks with the rest of the sugar until light and fluffy. Pour the infused milk into the egg mixture and stir with a spatula. Pour the mixture into a clean pan and heat gently, stirring continuously, until it is thick enough to coat the back of a wooden spoon: do not allow it to boil or the mixture will curdle. Remove the vanilla bean and pass the mixture through a fine sieve into a bowl. Fold in the white chocolate.

5 Pour the mixture into an ice cream maker, churn, and, when the ice cream starts to freeze, add the chili mixture, churn for a further 2 minutes, then freeze. If making by hand, pour the mixture into a freezer-proof container then freeze for 40 minutes. Remove from the freezer, whisk to break up any ice crystals, stir in the chili mixture, then refreeze. Repeat this process for the next $2\frac{1}{2}$ hours then freeze until firm.

6 Leave the ice cream to soften for 5–10 minutes then serve in scoops.

Ingredients
4 tbsp water
1 cup superfine sugar
2 tsp seeded and finely diced red jalapeño chili
$1^{2}/_{3}$ cups heavy cream
$1^{2}/_{3}$ cups lowfat milk
1 vanilla bean, split
11oz white chocolate, broken into pieces
8 standard egg yolks

Makes about 4 cups

Chocolate arlequin

THE LAYERS OF RICH WHITE AND DARK CHOCOLATE MOUSSE MAKE
THIS FRENCH-INSPIRED DESSERT A MUST FOR CHOCOLATE LOVERS.

1 Preheat the oven to 350°F. Line a 10- x 8- x 2-inch deep baking sheet with baking parchment, then butter and flour.

2 To make the sponge, whisk the eggs and superfine sugar together until light and pale. Sift the flour into the bowl then fold in carefully with a spatula. Pour into the prepared baking sheet, level with a spatula, and bake for 20–25 minutes until risen and golden. Remove from the oven and leave the sponge in the pan for 10 minutes then turn out on to a wire rack to cool.

3 Next, to make the chocolate cream, melt the chocolate in a heatproof bowl placed over a saucepan of gently simmering water, then set aside to cool slightly. Fold the crème pâtissière into the melted chocolate then fold in the whipped cream. Repeat this method to make the white chocolate cream.

4 Trim the edges of the sponge base then slice horizontally. Using a 3$\frac{1}{2}$-inch flan ring cut the sponge into sixteen $\frac{1}{2}$-inch thick rounds. Put a sponge base into the bottom of one of 8 individual flan rings. Drizzle over a little of the brandy. Spoon over the dark chocolate cream until the mold is half full. Place a second layer of sponge on top. Gently push down then fill the mold with the white chocolate cream and smooth the top. Repeat to make seven more desserts then chill for 4–6 hours.

5 Remove the flan rings with the aid of a kitchen blowtorch or wrap a hot cloth around the ring. If liked, gently mottle the top of each dessert with a blowtorch. If using a blowtorch, return the desserts to the fridge to chill. Serve decorated with orange segments, shaved white chocolate, and fresh mint.

Ingredients
butter, for greasing
2$\frac{1}{4}$ cups all-purpose flour, plus extra for dusting
8 standard eggs
1$\frac{1}{4}$ cups superfine sugar
$\frac{1}{2}$ tsp vanilla extract
1$\frac{1}{2}$ tbsp brandy

For the dark chocolate cream:
6oz bittersweet or semisweet chocolate, broken
  into pieces
$\frac{1}{2}$ quantity crème pâtissière (see page 18)
scant 1$\frac{1}{2}$ cups heavy cream, whipped

For the white chocolate cream:
6oz white chocolate, broken into pieces
$\frac{1}{2}$ quantity crème pâtissière (see page 18)
scant 1$\frac{1}{2}$ cups heavy cream, whipped

To decorate:
orange segments
white chocolate shavings (see page 8)
fresh mint leaves

Serves 8

Something chocolate

SINCE OPENING OUR RESTAURANT, THIS RECIPE REMAINS A FIRM
FAVORITE. IT REALLY IS VERY SIMPLE TO PREPARE AND IS BEST LEFT AT
ROOM TEMPERATURE FOR A FEW MINUTES BEFORE YOU SERVE.

Ingredients
4$^{1}/_{2}$oz bittersweet or semisweet chocolate, broken into pieces
4$^{1}/_{2}$oz milk chocolate, broken into pieces
1 cup heavy cream

To serve:
1 mango, peeled, pitted, and finely chopped
1 cup raspberries
3 tbsp melted bittersweet chocolate
4 small pieces of bubble wrap chocolate (see page 8)

Serves 4

1 Melt both types of chocolate in a heatproof bowl placed
over a saucepan of gently simmering water. Leave to cool
slightly.

2 Half whip the cream – do not whip to a full peak as the
cream needs to be carefully folded into the chocolate –
then fold into the chocolate until combined.

3 Spoon the chocolate mixture into 4 paper cones (like the
ones used in drinking water fountains) or 1-cup ramekins,
tap to remove any excess air and smooth over the top. If
you are using the paper cones, place each one in a plastic
cup to keep it upright. Refrigerate the cones or ramekins
until the chocolate is set; this will take about 3 hours.

4 Meanwhile, make the fruit sauces. Put the mango in a
blender and process until puréed. Press the mango sauce
through a sieve to remove any fibers. Repeat this process
to make the raspberry sauce.

5 To remove the chocolate from the cones, quickly
submerge each cone in warm water and carefully unpeel.
To serve, place a cone or ramekin in the center of each
serving plate, paint strips of melted chocolate on the plate,
and drizzle with the mango and raspberry sauces. Finally,
place a piece of bubble wrap chocolate on top of each
cone or ramekin.

Chocolate Bavarian cream

THIS REVIVED CLASSIC IS POPULAR IN OUR RESTAURANT, IT LOOKS GOOD DECORATED WITH PIPED CREAM.

Ingredients

light olive oil, for greasing
3 standard eggs, separated
3 1/2 tbsp superfine sugar
1 cup milk
1 vanilla bean, split and seeds scraped out (optional)
3 gelatin leaves, soaked in water
2oz bittersweet, semisweet, or milk chocolate, broken into pieces
scant 1 1/4 cups heavy cream, plus extra to decorate
chocolate pistoles or buttons, to decorate
cocoa powder, for dusting

Serves 6

1 Lightly oil six 2/3-cup ramekins. In a mixing bowl, whisk the egg yolks and sugar together until light and fluffy.

2 Put the milk and vanilla bean and seeds, if using, in a saucepan and bring up to a boil. Pour the milk into the egg mixture, stir, and transfer the mixture to a clean pan. Heat gently, stirring continuously, until the mixture thickens enough to coat the back of a wooden spoon; do not allow to boil or the mixture will curdle. Remove the vanilla bean.

3 Squeeze the soaked gelatin leaves to remove any excess water and add to the custard mixture. Stir until the gelatin dissolves.

4 Pass the custard through a fine sieve into a bowl containing the chocolate. Stir well until the chocolate is melted. Allow the mixture to cool; this is best achieved when placed over a bowl of iced water.

5 Whisk the egg whites until they form soft peaks then whisk in the cream.

6 The chocolate mixture will start to set after a few minutes. At this point, gently fold in the egg white mixture; do not whisk as you do not want air bubbles in the bavarois. Pour the mixture into the prepared ramekins and chill for 3–4 hours until set.

7 To serve, briefly place the basins in hot water. Carefully loosen the sides of the bavarois from the basins and turn out. Decorate the base with piped whipped cream, chocolate pistoles or buttons, and dust with cocoa.

White chocolate mousse with passionfruit swirl

THIS INDULGENT MOUSSE IS SO LIGHT AND FLUFFY AND IS JUST AS DELICIOUS WITH CRUSHED FRESH RASPBERRIES OR BLACKBERRIES SWIRLED IN.

Ingredients
9oz white chocolate, broken into pieces
5 tbsp milk
1 vanilla bean, split and seeds scraped out
3 standard eggs, separated
1½ cups heavy cream, whipped
4 passionfruit, halved and seeds scooped out
shredded fresh mint, to decorate (optional)

Serves 6

1 Put the chocolate and milk in a heatproof bowl placed over a saucepan of gently simmering water. Heat until the chocolate is just melted, stirring regularly. Stir the vanilla seeds into the mixture then leave to cool for 5 minutes.

2 Next, add the egg yolks, one at a time, beating well between each addition.

3 Fold the whipped cream into the chocolate mixture.

4 Whisk the egg whites until they form soft peaks, then fold half into the chocolate mixture, followed by the remaining half.

5 Divide the mousse between 6 individual serving bowls, then swirl the passionfruit pulp over the top of each bowl. Cover and chill for 3–4 hours until set. Decorate with mint before serving.

Chocolate tiramisu

THIS IS OUR BRASSERIE-STYLE VERSION OF THE CLASSIC ITALIAN DESSERT. SERVE IN INDIVIDUAL GLASSES OR, FAMILY-STYLE, SPOONED FROM A LARGE BOWL.

Ingredients
6 tbsp superfine sugar
6½ tbsp water
4 tbsp Madeira
7oz bittersweet or semisweet chocolate, broken into pieces
7oz milk chocolate, broken into pieces
6 standard eggs, separated
2lb 4oz mascarpone
14oz ladyfingers, broken into pieces or cubed
cocoa powder, for dusting

Serves 6–8

1 Put half of the sugar and water in a small saucepan and bring to a boil, stir in the Madeira, then leave to cool.

2 Melt the dark and milk chocolate in a heatproof bowl placed over a saucepan of gently simmering water. Leave to cool slightly.

3 Whisk the egg yolks and remaining superfine sugar together until light and fluffy. Beat in the mascarpone until combined. Carefully fold the mascarpone mixture into the melted chocolate.

4 Whisk the egg whites until they form soft peaks then fold into the chocolate mixture.

5 Place half the ladyfingers in the bottom of serving glasses or in a large serving bowl. Pour half the Madeira syrup over the ladyfingers. Cover with the mascarpone mixture. Repeat with another layer of ladyfingers, syrup, and mascarpone.

6 Chill then dust with cocoa powder before serving.

Pictured on page 1

Chocolate marquise

DURING THE SUMMER MONTHS WE ARE INUNDATED WITH FRESH BERRIES. YOU CAN USE RASPBERRIES, BLACK CURRANTS, STRAWBERRIES, OR BLUEBERRIES – OR A MIX OF EVERYTHING – AS PART OF THE FILLING IN THIS DECADENT CHOCOLATE JELLY ROLL.

1 Preheat the oven to 350°F. Press half of the raspberries through a sieve or purée in a blender to make a smooth sauce. If blending, press through a sieve afterwards to remove the seeds.

2 In a clean mixing bowl, whisk the egg yolks with half of the confectioners' sugar until light and fluffy. In a separate bowl, whisk the egg whites until they form soft peaks then gradually add the remaining sugar and whisk until stiff. Stir the two egg mixtures together using a metal spoon. Add the cornstarch and cocoa powder and fold until combined.

3 Line a 10½- x 9½-inch baking sheet with baking parchment, then grease lightly with butter and dust with flour. Spread the roulade mixture in an even layer, about ½-inch thick, to cover the base of the tray. Bake for 8–12 minutes until risen and the mixture springs back when pressed – do not worry if it feels slightly soft as it needs to be for rolling later.

4 Turn the roulade out on to a clean, damp cloth; carefully remove the paper (if this proves difficult, dampen the paper with a little water and carefully peel off) and neatly trim the edges.

5 Allow the roulade to cool slightly. Smear the raspberry sauce (setting some aside to serve) over the roulade, then top with the whipped cream and level with a spatula. Liberally scatter the raspberries (setting some aside to serve) over the cream. Now comes the fun bit!

6 Very carefully, from the short end, roll up the roulade using the damp cloth as a guide. Leave the roulade wrapped in the cloth and set aside to chill.

7 When you are ready to serve, carefully remove the cloth and slice the roulade on the diagonal. Serve with the reserved raspberries and raspberry sauce and decorate with fresh mint.

Ingredients

1¼ cups raspberries
6 standard eggs, separated
2¼ cups confectioners' sugar, sifted
4 tbsp cornstarch, sifted
scant 1 cup cocoa powder, sifted
butter, for greasing
flour, for dusting
1¼ cups heavy cream, whipped
fresh mint leaves, to decorate

Serves 10

Chocolate and ginger terrine with cinnamon custard

A SIMPLE CLASSIC COMBINATION OF CHOCOLATE TRUFFLE WITH STEM GINGER, SERVED WITH A PERFUMED, LIGHT CINNAMON CUSTARD. A GREAT MARRIAGE!

Ingredients

For the terrine:
9oz bittersweet or semisweet chocolate, broken into pieces
9oz milk chocolate, broken into pieces
2 pieces of stem ginger in syrup, finely chopped
2 1/4 cups heavy cream, whipped

For the custard:
2 1/4 cups milk
1 vanilla bean, split and seeds scraped out
1/2 cup superfine sugar
6 standard egg yolks
1 tsp ground cinnamon

Serves 6

1 Melt the dark and milk chocolate together in a heatproof bowl placed over a saucepan of gently simmering water. Mix in the chopped stem ginger then allow to cool slightly. Fold the whipped cream into the chocolate mixture.

2 Line a 1lb loaf pan or small terrine mold with plastic wrap. Pour the chocolate mixture into the prepared pan or mold. Cover and chill in the fridge for at least 3 hours until set.

3 To make the custard, heat the milk with the vanilla bean and seeds and half of the sugar up to boiling point, stirring occasionally. Meanwhile, whisk the egg yolks with the remaining sugar and cinnamon until light and fluffy.

4 Whisk the hot milk into the egg mixture and return it to the saucepan. Heat gently, stirring continuously, until the custard thickens enough to coat the back of a wooden spoon; do not allow it to boil or the mixture will curdle. Pass through a fine sieve then cool and chill.

5 To serve, gently turn out the terrine, carefully remove the plastic wrap and slice using a hot knife. Place a slice of the terrine on a serving plate and drizzle around the custard.

Chef's note: To serve the terrine in the chocolate box, pictured, melt 9oz bittersweet or semisweet chocolate following the instructions for White and milk chocolate garnish, page 9. Before serving each slice of the terrine, use a hot knife to cut the chocolate into rectangles the appropriate size. Prop the chocolate around the terrine slice and pipe chocolate into the corners and around the base of the box to secure.

Cakes and pastries

Dark chocolate truffle cake

THIS IS SIMPLICITY ON A PLATE – MILK AND BITTERSWEET OR SEMISWEET CHOCOLATE WITH WHIPPED CREAM – SMOOTH, RICH AND CREAMY. PURE INDULGENCE!

Ingredients
8oz bittersweet or semisweet chocolate, broken into pieces
1¼ cups heavy cream
cocoa powder, for dusting

Serves 4–6

1 Melt the chocolate in a heatproof bowl placed over a saucepan of gently simmering water.

2 Gently heat the cream then stir it into the melted chocolate.

3 Pour the mixture into a 8-inch loose-bottomed, non-stick flan ring on a flat plate and leave to set for 3 hours in the refrigerator.

4 To remove the ring, heat the edges with a blowtorch for 30 seconds or dip a thin, bladed knife in boiling water and run it around the inside of the ring. Use the back of the knife to smooth the edges. Dust with cocoa powder.

Dark chocolate and marmalade tart

THIS IMPRESSIVE TART HAS A FANTASTIC COMBINATION OF FLAVORS: THE MARMALADE WORKS EXCEPTIONALLY WELL WITH THE CHOCOLATE, WHILE THE MASCARPONE ADDS A RICH CREAMINESS.

Ingredients
2¼ cups all-purpose flour, sifted
scant 1 cup confectioners' sugar, sifted
2 standard egg yolks
4 drops vanilla extract
cocoa powder, for dusting
mascarpone and pieces of Milk and white chocolate decoration (see page 9), to decorate

For the filling:
scant 1 cup unsalted butter, cubed
10½ oz bittersweet or semisweet chocolate, broken into pieces
¼ cup superfine sugar
2 standard eggs, plus 2 additional standard egg yolks
½ cup thick-cut marmalade

Serve 4–6

1 First make the sweet pastry case, place the flour and butter in a food processor and process until fine crumbs. Transfer to a bowl and mix in the confectioners' sugar.

2 Beat the egg yolks and vanilla extract together in a bowl and add to the pastry mixture. Bring the pastry together, wrap in plastic wrap, and allow to rest in the fridge for 1 hour.

3 Preheat the oven to 350°F. Grease a 9-inch loose-bottomed flan pan. Remove the pastry from the fridge, roll out, then press the pastry into the pan. Chill for 20 minutes. Trim the edges then line the pastry with baking parchment, fill with baking beans, and bake blind for 15–20 minutes or until the sides of the pastry are golden. Remove the parchment and beans and allow to cool. Reduce the oven to 325°F.

4 To make the filling, melt the butter and chocolate together in a heatproof bowl placed over a saucepan of gently simmering water, stir until combined. Whisk together the sugar, eggs, and additional egg yolks, then fold into the chocolate mixture.

5 Spoon the marmalade into the pastry case and spread out evenly. Pour the chocolate mixture into the case, level, and bake for 15 minutes. Remove the tart from the oven and cool on a wire rack. Dust the tart with cocoa powder then remove from the pan. To serve, slice the tart with a hot knife and top each slice with a spoonful of mascarpone and a piece of milk and white chocolate.

Previous page: Dark chocolate truffle cake
Opposite: Dark chocolate and marmalade tart

1 Preheat the oven to 425°F. Lightly grease a 6-hole, non-stick muffin pan.

2 Put the egg yolks, sugar, and cornstarch into a bowl and whisk until light and fluffy. Add the cream and water then whisk again. Pour the mixture into a saucepan with the vanilla bean and seeds. Heat over a medium heat, stirring continuously with a wooden spoon, for about 5 minutes until the mixture thickens.

3 Remove from the heat, add the chocolate, and stir until the chocolate is melted. Leave to cool.

4 Roll out the pastry on a floured work surface until ½-inch thick. Using a pastry cutter, cut six 4-inch rounds then press each pastry round into a muffin pan hole. Place in a freezer and chill for 10 minutes.

5 Next, fold the pistachios into the chocolate custard. Remove the muffin tray from the freezer and divide the chocolate custard between the tart shells and smooth the tops. Bake for 20 minutes until the pastry is golden.

6 Remove from the oven and cool on a wire rack for 10 minutes before removing the tarts from the muffin trays. Sprinkle with additional pistachios before serving.

Ingredients

butter, for greasing
4 standard egg yolks
¼ cup superfine sugar
2 tbsp cornstarch
scant 1 cup heavy cream
½ cup water
1 vanilla bean, split and seeds scraped out
5½oz bittersweet or semisweet chocolate, grated
7oz sheet puff pastry
¼ cup peeled and chopped pistachios, plus extra for sprinkling

Makes 6

Chocolate and pistachio custard tarts

THESE INDIVIDUAL TARTS, WITH THEIR INTENSELY CHOCOLATEY CUSTARD, PISTACHIOS, AND RICH PASTRY SHELL, MAKE THE PERFECT AFTERNOON TREAT.

Chocolate birthday cake

ENJOY THIS IMPRESSIVE LAYERED CHOCOLATE CAKE – IT'S A MASSIVE
FAVORITE AT CHILDREN'S BIRTHDAY PARTIES.

Ingredients
butter, for greasing
$3/4$ cup all-purpose flour, plus extra for dusting
scant 1 cup raspberries
4 standard eggs
generous $1/2$ cup superfine sugar
$1/4$ cup cocoa powder

For the chocolate cream:
$2^1/3$ cups heavy cream
$1/4$ cup cocoa powder
$1/4$ cup confectioners' sugar

To decorate:
chocolate pistoles or buttons
piped chocolate (see page 9)
whipped cream

Serves 10

1 Preheat the oven to 350°F. Butter and flour a 10-inch cake pan. To make the raspberry purée, blend the raspberries in a blender or press through a sieve. If blending, press through a sieve to remove any seeds.

2 In a bowl, whisk the eggs and superfine sugar together until light and pale. Sift the flour and cocoa powder into the bowl then fold in carefully with a spatula. Pour into the prepared cake pan and bake for 20–25 minutes until risen. Remove from the oven and leave in the pan for 10 minutes then turn out on to a wire rack to cool.

3 To make the chocolate cream, pour the heavy cream into a bowl and sift in the cocoa powder and confectioners' sugar then whisk the mixture until thick and creamy.

4 Cut the cake into 3 horizontal layers, and place one layer on a serving plate. Spoon half of the raspberry purée over the cake, add a large spoonful of the chocolate cream, and spread it all over. Repeat with a second layer of sponge, raspberry purée, and cream.

5 Place the remaining layer of sponge on top and press down gently. Using a spatula, spread the remaining chocolate cream around the sides of the cake and over the top. Smooth and level the chocolate cream with a warm metal spatula.

6 To decorate, pipe chocolate cream and whipped cream around the base and top of the cake. Pipe chocolate over the cream then arrange chocolate pistoles or buttons on top. Personalise the cake with piped chocolate, if liked (see page 9).

Dreamy chocolate and orange cake

THE ULTIMATE COMBINATION OF CHOCOLATE AND ORANGE, THIS FOOLPROOF CAKE
MAKES AN EXCELLENT DINNER PARTY DESSERT OR AFTERNOON TREAT.

Ingredients

9oz bittersweet or semisweet chocolate, broken into pieces
generous 1 cup unsalted butter, cut into small pieces, plus
    extra for greasing
2 tbsp orange zest
6 standard eggs, separated
generous $\frac{1}{2}$ cup superfine sugar
3 tbsp all-purpose flour, sifted
$\frac{1}{4}$ cup ground almonds

To decorate:

cocoa powder, for dusting
orange slices and grated orange zest
mint leaves, torn
crème fraîche or heavy cream

Serves 6–8

1 Preheat the oven to 375°F. Lightly grease a 9-inch spring-form cake pan. Melt the chocolate and butter with the orange zest in a heatproof bowl placed over a saucepan of gently simmering water. When just melted, stir the mixture and set aside.

2 Whisk the egg yolks with the sugar until light and fluffy. Gradually pour the melted chocolate into the egg mixture, stirring constantly. Next, take a large spoon and fold in the flour and ground almonds.

3 Put the egg whites into a clean bowl and whisk until they form stiff peaks. Using a large metal spoon, fold the egg whites into the chocolate mixture until they are just combined. Pour the mixture into the prepared pan and bake for 35 minutes – the cake will be very moist in the center but avoid cooking it for any longer.

4 Remove the cake from the oven and leave to cool completely in the pan. Transfer the cake to a serving plate and dust with cocoa then decorate with orange slices and zest, fresh mint, and spoonfuls of crème fraîche or heavy cream.

Chocolate and blue cheese tart

BELIEVE IT OR NOT, CHOCOLATE AND BLUE CHEESE ARE A MATCH MADE IN HEAVEN AS SHOWN IN THIS UNUSUAL BUT TRULY SUPERB, DECADENT DESSERT.

Ingredients

For the pastry:
2$^1/_4$ cups all-purpose flour
$^3/_4$ tsp salt
1$^1/_2$ tsp confectioners' sugar
9 tbsp unsalted butter, diced
1 standard egg, lightly beaten
$^1/_4$ cup water

For the filling:
7oz bittersweet or semisweet chocolate, broken
   into pieces
10 tbsp unsalted butter, melted
$^1/_3$ cup all-purpose flour
3 standard eggs
scant $^1/_4$ cup superfine sugar
1$^1/_4$ cups Stilton or Roquefort blue cheese, crumbled

Serves 4

1 Sift the flour into a bowl then mix in the salt and sugar. Rub the butter into the flour until the mixture resembles fine bread crumbs. Mix in the egg and water and form into a dough. Knead until smooth.

2 Lay out a large piece of plastic wrap, place the dough on top, fold over the plastic wrap and press the pastry out flat. Chill for 20 minutes. Lightly butter four 4-inch fluted, loose-bottomed flan pans.

3 On a floured work surface, roll out the pastry until about $^1/_8$-inch thick. Cut out four 4$^1/_2$-inch rounds and carefully press into the prepared flan pans, leaving any excess pastry overlapping the sides. Chill in the fridge for 20 minutes.

4 Meanwhile, preheat the oven to 350°F. To make the filling, gently melt the chocolate and butter together in a heatproof bowl placed over a saucepan of gently simmering water. Stir until combined then leave to cool.

5 Line the pastry cases with baking parchment, fill with baking beans, and bake blind for 15–20 minutes or until the sides of the pastry are golden. Leave to cool on a wire rack. Remove the paper and beans from the pans then carefully trim the edges.

6 Increase the oven to 375°F. Whisk the eggs and sugar together until light and fluffy. Add the cooled chocolate and butter, then fold in the flour. Pour the mixture into the pastry molds, almost up to the top. Sprinkle the cheese over the top then bake for 8–10 minutes. Leave to cool then carefully remove the tarts from the pans.

Small bites

Chocolate tuiles

A PRETTY, CRISP COOKIE THAT LOOKS LIKE A CURVED TILE. SERVE AFTER A MEAL WITH COFFEE OR AS AN ACCOMPANIMENT TO A DESSERT.

Ingredients
5 tbsp unsalted butter, softened, plus extra for greasing
2 tbsp clear wildflower honey
1 cup confectioners' sugar
generous $3/4$ cup all-purpose flour
generous $1/4$ cup cocoa powder
1 standard egg white

Makes about 20

1 Preheat the oven to 350°F. Line a large baking sheet with baking parchment. Place the butter and honey in a mixing bowl and beat using an electric hand mixer until smooth and creamy.

2 Sift the sugar, flour, and cocoa powder together then gradually whisk into the creamed mixture. Mix well until incorporated. At a low speed gradually add the egg white. When mixed in, increase the speed to high and whisk for 5 minutes until a smooth paste.

3 Spoon a tablespoon of the chocolate mixture on to the prepared baking sheet. Using the back of a dessertspoon, spread the mixture into a $3^1/4$-inch diameter circle, about $1/8$-inch thick. Repeat this process until the baking sheet is covered in rounds or 'tuiles'. Bake for 4–5 minutes until slightly firm.

4 Leave to rest for 30 seconds. Remove the tuiles from the baking sheet using a spatula and when still warm, drape each one over a lightly greased rolling pin and leave until cool and crisp. Work quickly as the mixture will set almost immediately. Alternatively, mold each tuile over an inverted coffee mug or cup to make a chocolate basket. If you need to, pop the tuiles back in the oven to soften then resume shaping.

Chocolate chip cookies

THESE SERIOUSLY CHOCOLATEY COOKIES SHOULD STILL BE SOFT AND GOOEY IN THE CENTER WHEN THEY COME OUT OF THE OVEN.

Ingredients
8 tbsp unsalted butter, plus extra for greasing
$3^1/2$ tbsp superfine sugar
$3^1/2$ tbsp soft brown sugar
1 standard egg
$1/2$ tsp vanilla extract
$1^1/4$ cups all-purpose flour
$1/2$ tsp baking soda
1 cup semisweet or bittersweet chocolate chips
$1^1/2$ tbsp chopped walnuts (optional)

Makes about 20

1 Preheat the oven to 350°F and lightly butter a baking sheet. Beat the butter and both types of sugar together in a large mixing bowl until light and creamy. Whisk in the egg and vanilla extract.

2 In a smaller bowl, sift the flour and baking soda together. Gradually add this to the sugar and egg mixture and beat until smooth. Fold in the chocolate chips and chopped walnuts, if using.

3 Spoon a tablespoon (or teaspoon if making smaller cookies) of the mixture at well-spaced intervals on to the prepared baking sheet or tray. Bake for about 10 minutes until golden. Leave to cool slightly then transfer to a wire rack to cool.

Previous page: Chocolate tuiles
Opposite: Chocolate chip cookies

Whisky truffles

PERFECT WITH COFFEE FOLLOWING A MEAL, THESE CHOCOLATE TRUFFLES ARE SO SIMPLE TO MAKE. YOU COULD ALSO USE YOUR FAVORITE SPIRIT INSTEAD OF SCOTCH WHISKY.

Ingredients
scant $\frac{1}{2}$ cup heavy cream
12oz bittersweet or semisweet chocolate, broken
  into pieces
scant 1 cup confectioners' sugar, sifted
4 tbsp Scotch whisky, warmed
scant 1 cup cocoa powder, for dusting

Makes about 20

1 Line a large baking sheet with baking parchment. Bring the cream up to a boil in a saucepan then remove from the heat and stir in the chocolate pieces. Whisk until smooth, then whisk in the confectioners' sugar.

2 Pour in the warm whisky and whisk again until smooth. Pour the mixture into a mixing bowl, cover with plastic wrap, and chill for about 6 hours until set.

3 When the mixture is set, dust a plate and your hands with cocoa powder. Divide the chocolate mixture into 20 equal portions – about the size of a walnut – and roll into balls in the palm of your hand. Roll the balls in the cocoa powder and leave to firm up in the fridge. Before serving, place the truffles in petit four cases.

Mocha swirls

THESE BITE-SIZED MORSELS MELT IN THE MOUTH AND HAVE A SLIGHT HINT OF COFFEE. THEY'RE GREAT WITH TEA, COFFEE, OR, OF COURSE, WITH OUR HOT CHOCOLATE, SEE PAGE 60.

Ingredients

2oz milk chocolate, broken into pieces
2oz bittersweet or semisweet chocolate, broken into pieces
scant 1 cup unsalted butter, softened
4 tbsp confectioners' sugar, sifted
1 tbsp instant coffee granules
$1\frac{3}{4}$ cups all-purpose flour, sifted
4 tbsp cornstarch, sifted

Makes 30 swirls

1 Preheat the oven to 350°F. Line a large baking sheet with baking parchment.

2 Melt the milk and bittersweet or semisweet chocolate in a heatproof bowl placed over a saucepan of gently simmering water; stir gently until combined.

3 In a mixing bowl, whisk the butter and confectioners' sugar together until light and pale.

4 Mix the coffee with 1 tablespoon boiling water and set aside. Add the melted chocolate to the butter and sugar mixture, and stir until incorporated. Add the diluted coffee then fold in the flour and cornstarch.

5 Spoon the mixture into a pastry bag with a star tube and pipe $1\frac{1}{4}$-inch rounds onto the prepared baking sheet. Bake for 8–10 minutes – the cookies should still be very soft. Remove from the oven and leave the swirls on the baking sheet for 5–10 minutes then transfer to a wire rack to cool. The swirls can be stored in an airtight container for up to 5 days.

Dark chocolate fruit and nut bars

ADAPTED FROM THE BRITISH FAVORITE CHOCOLATE FRUIT AND NUT BAR,
THIS IS A RICHER ALTERNATIVE AND TRULY MELTS IN THE MOUTH.

1 Line a 10½- x 12½- x 1-inch deep baking sheet with baking parchment. Melt the chocolate and butter in a heatproof bowl placed over a saucepan of gently simmering water; stir until combined.

2 Fold the remaining ingredients into the chocolate and butter and mix until combined.

3 Spoon the mixture into the prepared baking sheet and spread into an even layer, about ¾-inch deep, using a spatula. Allow to set in the refrigerator for 4–5 hours. Remove from the tray and cut into bite-sized pieces.

Ingredients

7oz bittersweet or semisweet chocolate,
  broken into pieces
scant ½ cup unsalted butter, cubed
11oz sweetened condensed milk
5½oz gingernut cookies, crushed
1½ cups dried apricots, chopped
1¾ cups pecans, chopped
scant 1 cup macadamia nuts, chopped

Makes about 40

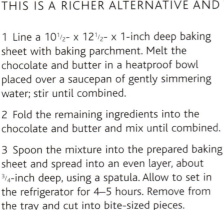

Coconut crunch

SMOOTH, CREAMY CHOCOLATE AND CRUNCHY COCONUT
GIVES THIS COOKIE A TRUE TASTE OF PARADISE.

1 Line a $10^{1}/_{2}$- x $12^{1}/_{2}$- x 1-inch deep baking
sheet with baking parchment. Melt the
chocolate and butter together in a heatproof
bowl placed over a saucepan of gently
simmering water then stir until combined

2 Fold the remaining ingredients into the
chocolate and butter and mix until combined.

3 Spoon the mixture into the prepared baking
sheet and spread into an even layer, about
$^{3}/_{4}$-inch deep, using a spatula. Allow to set in
the refrigerator for 4–5 hours. Remove from
the tray and cut into squares.

Ingredients
7oz bittersweet or semisweet chocolate,
  broken into pieces
scant $^{1}/_{2}$ cup unsalted butter, cubed
12oz sweetened condensed milk
$2^{1}/_{2}$ cups grated coconut, toasted
scant 1 cup dried glacé cherries, chopped

Makes about 20

Sauces and drinks

Vanilla and cinnamon hot chocolate

THIS IS A FABULOUS WINTER WARMER BUT TO BE HONEST, IT'S GREAT
AT ANY TIME. YOU CAN ALWAYS ADD A SHOT OF YOUR FAVORITE
TIPPLE – BAILEY'S WORKS EXCEPTIONALLY WELL.

Ingredients
4 cups milk
1/2 vanilla bean, split and seeds scraped out
1/2 cup cocoa powder, plus extra for dusting
4 tbsp superfine sugar
1/4 tsp cinnamon

To serve:
bittersweet or semisweet chocolate buttons
whipped cream

Serves 4

1 Carefully warm the milk and vanilla seeds in a saucepan, taking care not to let it boil. Remove the warm milk from the heat and whisk in the cocoa, sugar, and cinnamon.

2 Place a few chocolate buttons in the bottom of 4 cups or paint melted chocolate inside the base of the glass. Pour in the hot chocolate. Spoon the whipped cream on top, then dust with cocoa, and serve.

Hot chocolate with sage

CHOCOLATE WITH SAGE IS A FANTASTIC COMBINATION – YOU GET
A SUBTLE KICK OF THE HERB AFTER THE INITIAL CHOCOLATE SENSATION.

Ingredients
4 cups whole milk
4 tbsp superfine sugar
5 tbsp cocoa powder, plus extra for dusting
5 large fresh sage leaves, plus extra, to decorate (optional)

Serves 4

1 Carefully warm the milk with the sage leaves. Remove from the heat and allow to infuse for 1 hour. Pass the milk through a sieve and discard the sage leaves.

2 Return the milk to the saucepan with the sugar and cocoa powder and reheat, whisking well.

3 Whisk with a hand blender until frothy then pour into 4 heatproof glasses or mugs. Dust with cocoa and decorate with a sage leaf, if liked.

Previous page: Vanilla and cinnamon hot chocolate
Opposite: Hot chocolate with sage

Chocolate orange sauce

CHOCOLATE AND ORANGE ARE PERFECT
PARTNERS AS SHOWN IN THIS RICH,
AROMATIC SAUCE.

Ingredients
1 cup milk
zest of 1 grated orange
7oz bittersweet or semisweet chocolate, broken
   into pieces

Makes 1$\frac{1}{2}$ cups

Put the milk and orange zest in a saucepan and bring
up to a boil. Remove from the heat, add the chocolate,
and whisk until melted.

Bitter chocolate sauce

THIS RICH, DARK CHOCOLATE SAUCE
WORKS SURPRISINGLY WELL WITH SAVORY
DISHES. BITTER CHOCOLATE IS THE
PREFERRED TYPE TO USE, AT LEAST 55–75
PERCENT COCOA SOLIDS.

Ingredients
6 tbsp red wine
2 shallots, finely chopped
2$\frac{1}{2}$ cups fresh beef stock
1oz bittersweet chocolate buttons

Makes about scant 1 cup

1 Heat the red wine in a saucepan with the chopped
shallots and cook briskly until the wine is reduced by
half. Pour in the beef stock and cook over a medium-
high heat until reduced by two-thirds.

2 Remove from the heat and pass through a fine sieve.
Add the chocolate buttons and whisk until melted.

White chocolate sauce

THIS IS AN EXTREMELY EASY SAUCE TO MAKE
AND LOOKS IMPRESSIVE POURED OVER DARK
CHOCOLATE ICE CREAM.

Ingredients
1 cup milk
7oz white chocolate, broken into pieces

Makes about 1$\frac{1}{2}$ cups

Bring the milk up to a boil in a saucepan. Pour the hot milk
over the chocolate and stir well until melted.